MYSTERIES
OF THE RUBBER PEOPLE

By Stephanie Hanson
Illustrations by Matthew Maley

The Olmecs were first.

They had the first major civilization in Mexico.

They lived over 1500 years ago.

The Mayans and Aztecs got ideas from the Olmecs.

"Olmec" comes from an Aztec word.

It means "rubber people."

The Olmecs were artists.
They made giant heads.
They made masks out of jade.
They carved statues. The statues were life-size people.
They made ceramic babies.
They painted murals on cliffs.
They made plates and bowls out of pottery.
They made jade beads.
They made obsidian knives.

The Olmecs were athletes.

They had a ball game.

They played on ball courts.

They used a rubber ball.

They could not touch the ball with their hands.

They hit the ball with handstones.

They tried to get the ball through a ring.

Hundreds of people watched the games.

The Olmecs were religious.
They believed in were-jaguars.
They worshiped many gods.
They had a maize god.
They had a rain god.
They had a serpent god.
Many of their gods looked like animals.
There were eagles and cats.

They measured time.

They invented two calendars.

One had 260 days.

It followed the movement of the planet Venus.

One had 365 days.

It followed the sun.

The Mayans liked the Olmec calendars.

They made their own versions.

Some Mayans still use them today.

They were writers.
They had the first written language in Central America.
They used pictures to write.
The pictures are called glyphs.
They look like animals, plants, and everyday objects.
No one knows what they say.

They were traders.

They bought and sold goods over hundreds of miles.

They traded with other groups of people.

Jade came from the south.

Obsidian came from the north.

They traded magnetite mirrors.

They traded pottery.

They were rulers.

The giant heads might be carvings of kings.

The kings lived in palaces.

The palaces were in the middle of the cities.

There was a palace in San Lorenzo.

There was a palace in La Venta.

There was a palace in Tres Zapotes.

Each city had its own king.

They were builders.
They built pyramids.
They built thrones.
They built cities for worship.
They built mounds out of earth.
They built huge stone tables.

The Olmecs lived in houses.

Their houses were small.

They were fifteen feet long and nine feet wide.

The roofs were made of palm leaves.

The walls were made of poles.

The floors were made of dirt.

The Olmecs were hunters.
They hunted birds, rabbits, and deer.
They caught fish.
They ate frogs and turtles.

The Olmecs were inventors.

They invented rubber.

They used a tree sap called latex.

They mixed it with juice from morning glory vines.

They made shoes with rubber soles.

They made rubber balls.

They made rubber bands.

The Olmecs were farmers.
They grew corn.
They grew sunflowers.
They grew beans.
They grew cotton.
They stored root vegetables in pits.

The Olmecs were cooks.

They made tamales, tacos, and popcorn.

They cooked in pottery.

They cooked over fires.

They cooked in pits.

They drank hot chocolate.

What happened to the Olmecs?
Did their rivers dry up?
Did they have to move because of volcano eruptions?
Did they die from diseases?
We can only guess.

The Olmecs are a mystery.
We cannot read their writing.
We do not know what happened to them.
We do not know how they prayed.
We do not know why they made giant heads.
We don't know why they buried sculptures.
We don't know why they destroyed some of their art.
We do not know who was in charge.
We do not even know their real name.

CPSIA information can be obtained
at www.ICGtesting.com
Printed in the USA
LVHW071410120622
721088LV00018B/352

9 781956 571073